CHEMISTRY IN MEDICINE

Karolyn Kendrick

TABLE OF CONTENTS

Pictures To Think About

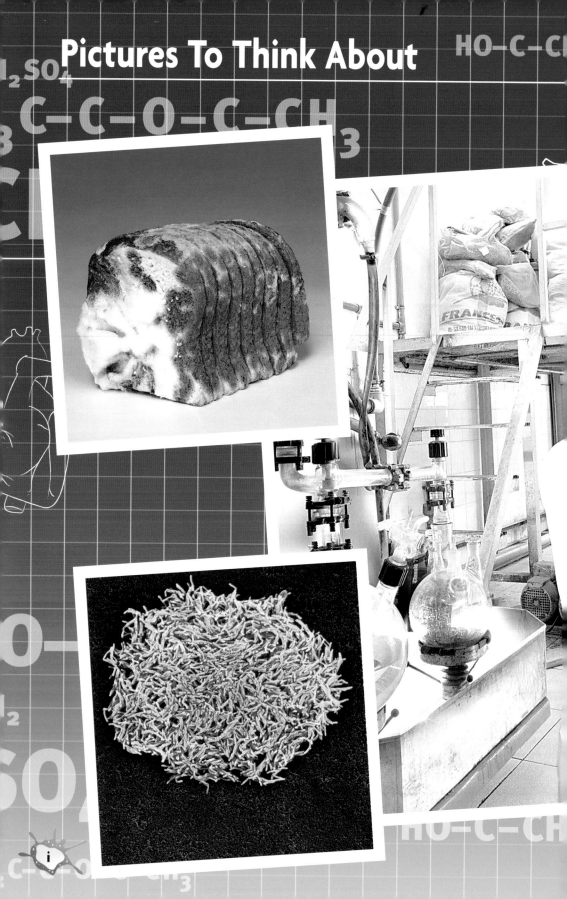

Words To Think About

Characteristics

type of drug

fights diseases

?

vaccine

What do you think the word **vaccine** means?

Examples

polio vaccine

measles vaccine

?

antibiotic

What do you think the word **antibiotic** means?

Greek: *anti* (against)

Greek: *biotikos* (fit for life)

iii

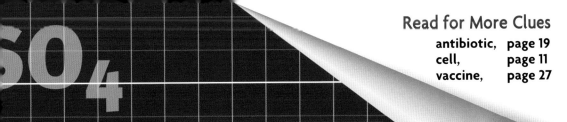

Read for More Clues

antibiotic, page 19
cell, page 11
vaccine, page 27

cell

What do you think the word **cell** means in this book?

Meaning 1
small room in a jail
(noun)

Meaning 2
building block of all living things
(noun)

Meaning 3
part of a battery
(noun)

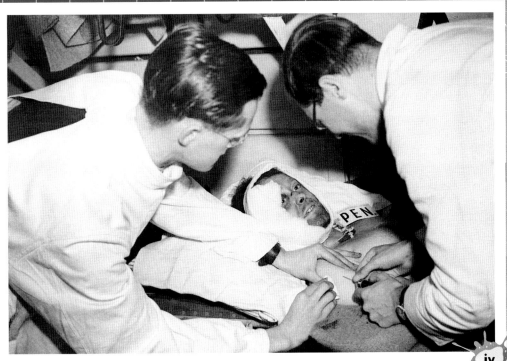

INTRODUCTION

Do you like to solve mysteries? Do you like to make discoveries? Then get ready. This book is about medical mysteries. It is also about discoveries that saved millions of lives.

For thousands of years, people have used plants as medicines. But people did not always know how plants help people.

In the 1800s, chemists began to study plants used for healing. They wanted to find out about the chemicals in the plants. This was the start of medical chemistry.

▲ Scientists make new discoveries in medicine each year.

▲ Many people still rely on plant medicines.

Scientists learned that **bacteria** (bak-TEER-ee-uh) and **viruses** (VY-rus-ez) cause disease. Bacteria are very tiny living things. You need a microscope to see them. Viruses are even smaller. Today, chemists can make drugs that attack bacteria and viruses.

Read on. Find out how aspirin works. See how a **fungus** (FUN-gus) saved lives. Find out how people still rely on plants for medicines. Learn about new drugs that came from rain forests. Then learn how scientists hope to stop the flu.

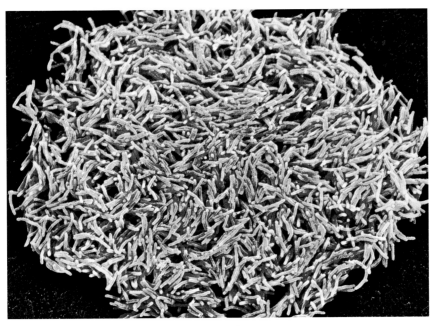

▲ This bacteria causes tuberculosis.

CHEMISTRY MATTERS

In this book, you will learn about chemistry. Here are some things you need to know.

- **Matter** (MA-ter) is anything that has mass and takes up space. Look in the mirror. *You* are matter.
- An **element** (EH-leh-ment) is a pure substance. It does not break down into something else. What makes balloons float? Can you guess? The element is helium (HEE-lee-um).
- **Atoms** (A-tumz) are the smallest bits of elements. Atoms join to form **molecules** (MAH-leh-kyoolz). Think of water. One molecule of water is made of two hydrogen (HY-druh-jen) atoms and one oxygen (AHK-sih-jen) atom. The symbol for water is H_2O.

▲ Water is made of two hydrogen atoms and one oxygen atom.

▲ The gas that fills these balloons is an element.

Observe the Differences Between Physical and Chemical Changes

▲ Physical changes happen all around you.

▲ Why do you think chemicals react?

WHAT YOU NEED

- pencil and paper
- an ice cube on a plate
- 1/2 teaspoon baking soda in a glass
- 1/4 cup (59 mL) vinegar

WHAT TO DO

1. Observe a physical change. Watch the ice cube melt. What change does the water undergo? Could you reverse the change? If so, how would you do that?

2. Observe a chemical reaction or change. Pour the vinegar on the baking soda. What happens to the baking soda? Can you reverse the change you observed?

TALK ABOUT IT

Use your observations to name one difference between physical and chemical changes.

THE STORY OF ASPIRIN

What does a willow tree have in common with an aspirin? The answer is that both contain the same substance.

Aspirin is the most used drug in the world. It helps stop headaches and other pains. Aspirin also helps prevent heart attacks. The story of aspirin begins with the willow tree.

For thousands of years, people used willow as a drug. The first known medical writings list willow leaves. Around 400 B.C.E., a famous Greek doctor told patients to chew willow bark. He said the bark would help cure fever and pain. Does this sound familiar?

▲ Today, doctors take a Hippocratic oath. It is named after Hippocrates. Doctors pledge to help their patients.

▲ Egyptian druggists squeezed animal skin filled with herbs to make herbal medicine.

In the 1820s, chemists studied willow bark. They wanted to know how it stopped pain. They ground up willow bark. Then they took out a bitter, yellow crystal from the bark.

They named the crystal salicin (SA-lih-sin). Then they changed salicin into salicylic (sa-lih-SIH-lik) acid. This is the pain-relieving chemical.

HISTORICAL PERSPECTIVE

In 1763, the Reverend Edward Stone gave willow bark tea to fifty patients. All had fevers. The willow tea reduced their fevers. This was one of the first clinical trials. It tested the drug's safety on humans. Today, all new drugs must go through careful clinical trials.

HO–C–CH

$_2SO_4$

THE WONDER DRUG

Everyone wanted salicylic acid. It made pain and fevers go away. But the drug was hard to get. The process people used to remove the acid was slow. It also cost a lot of money.

In the 1860s, chemists found an answer. The acid is a **compound** (KAHM-pownd). That means it has atoms from more than one element.

Chemists learned which atoms were in the acid. They no longer needed willow bark. Factories could make the drug cheaply.

It's a Fact

Chemical names are often very long. The official name for aspirin is acetylsalicylic acid (uh-SEE-tul-sa-lih-SIH-lik A-sid). What a mouthful! The names for salicin and salicylic acid both come from the word *salix*. That's the Latin name for *willow*.

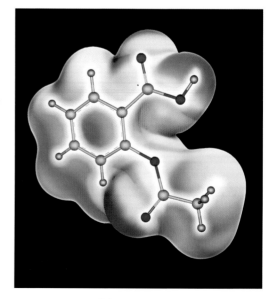

▲ aspirin molecule

O–C–CH$_3$

The chemists had a new problem, though. Some acids, such as lemon juice, are safe. They are mild. People can drink mild acids.

Salicylic acid is not mild. It is a stronger acid. It can burn the mouth and stomach. Many people could not use it. Bayer (BARE) is a German company. Bayer took on the task of making the acid safe.

THEY MADE A DIFFERENCE

Who created aspirin? Felix Hoffmann got all the credit. But Arthur Eichengrun may deserve credit, too. Eichengrun was Hoffmann's boss. He was also Jewish. Many people think the Nazis destroyed his part in the story. The Nazis came to power in 1933. They blamed Germany's problems on the Jews. They wiped out all records of their work.

Felix Hoffmann ▶

HO–C–CH

The Bayer chemists replaced one group of atoms. This made the acid change slightly. A new chemical formed.

The change made the drug less bitter. The drug did not burn as much. In 1899, Bayer named the new drug aspirin (AS-peh-ren). Soon, people around the world called aspirin the "wonder drug." Aspirin helped many people.

It's a Fact

Aspirin is probably a made-up word. The *a* stands for acetyl. That's the name of the new atom group. *Spir* comes from the name of a plant with salicylic acid. *In* was a common ending for names of medicines.

BAYER
PHARMACEUTICAL PRODUCTS.
We are now sending to Physicians throughout the United States literature and samples of

ASPIRIN

The substitute for the Salicylates, agreeable of taste, free from unpleasant after-effects.

The Sedative for Coughs,
H. HYDROCHLORIDE
Its water-soluble salt,
You will have call for them. Order a supply from your jobber.

Write for literature to
FARBENFABRIKEN OF ELBERFELD CO.
40 Stone Street, New York,
SELLING AGENTS.

▲ People around the world bought this new, amazing drug.

O–C–CH₃

Still, no one knew how aspirin worked. Why did it stop pain and reduce fevers?

In 1971, Dr. John Vane discovered how aspirin affects **cells** (SELZ). Cells are the building blocks of every living thing.

Here is how aspirin works. Suppose you hit your thumb with a hammer. Ouch! Your cells make chemicals that cause your thumb to swell. Your thumb turns red. Pain signals speed to your brain.

The chemicals in your body tell blood to rush to the wound. Your body starts to heal.

Aspirin stops cells from making the defense chemicals. That lowers pain. It also lowers swelling.

CAREERS CHEMIST

Chemists study how molecules are put together. They combine atoms in new ways to make new products. They make drugs, plastics, paints, cosmetics, and many other things we use. Biochemists study the chemicals in living things and how they interact.

▲ Chemicals in your cells tell your brain when you are in pain.

RAIN FOREST MEDICINES

Think of a tropical rain forest. It is warm and wet. Plants grow fast. Some plants grow very tall.

The rain forest has layers of life. At the top, giant trees reach for the sun. Smaller trees and vines form a canopy. Many animals live in the canopy. Much less sunlight enters the shady areas below.

On the ground, bacteria and fungi (FUN-jy) break down dead matter. Plants and other living things absorb, or take in, the **nutrients** (NOO-tree-ents). Nutrients help living things grow. In the crowded rain forest, every living thing is looking for a meal.

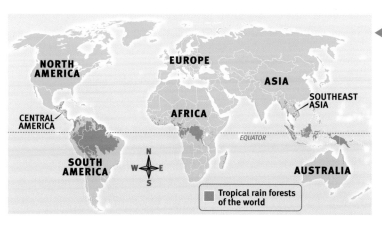

◀ Tropical rain forests are near the equator. They receive 80–400 inches (200–1,000 centimeters) of rain each year.

NORTH AMERICA

EUROPE

ASIA

SOUTHEAST ASIA

CENTRAL AMERICA

AFRICA

EQUATOR

SOUTH AMERICA

AUSTRALIA

N
W   E
S

Tropical rain forests of the world

Insects eat plant leaves. Fungi and bacteria invade wounded leaves. Monkeys and birds feed on leaves, flowers, and fruits.

Plants struggle to survive. They cannot run away. So plants have other defenses. Some plants make chemicals to protect themselves. How does this help us?

▲ Fungi like this can be found in the rain forest.

✓ POINT Reread

Reread the first two pages of this chapter. Which detail do you find most surprising? Why?

FINDING THE RIGHT PLANTS

More than one-quarter of the drugs we use are from plants. That is because the chemicals plants make to protect themselves also protect humans.

Finding the right plants is a hard job. The job is getting harder. Rain forests are in danger. Finding new plants is a race against time.

Some people think that rain forests are only good for lumber. Many people also want to farm land in rain forests. People cut and burn the forests. Each year, about 12,000 square miles (31,000 square kilometers) of the Amazon Rain Forest are lost. That is a huge area. It is about the size of Maryland.

Animals that live in rain forests are dying out. Many plants are dying out, too. Plants can save lives. Plants also help save rain forests. These plants show how priceless rain forests are.

▼ Burning, logging, and road-building destroy large areas of the rain forest.

Finding the plants is just the first step. Next, scientists must take out the plant chemicals. Then they test whether the chemicals fight disease.

Cancer occurs when cells grow out of control. Some scientists look for chemicals that stop cancer cells from growing. If a chemical kills cancer cells, it goes to the next test stage.

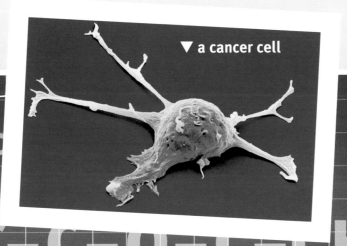

▼ a cancer cell

CAREERS ETHNOBOTANIST

Ethnobotanists study links between people and plants. They look at how different cultures use plants. Often, they talk to local healers. They learn about the plants the healers use as medicines. This is a way for scientists to find new plants that help cure disease.

▲ ethnobotanist

Next, scientists look at how the chemical works on living things. Then they try the chemical on people.

If the drug is safe, the government approves it.

Finally, it is okay for use. The process takes many years. Scientists test thousands of compounds. Only a few end up as drugs.

Q&A

Phyllis Coley studies plant defenses. She works in South America in the rain forests. She uses her knowledge to help develop drugs.

Q: How do you find plants with the right chemicals?

A: The insects tell us.

Q: How do they tell you?

A: We look for plants that insects don't eat. Baby leaves are tender and nutritious. So, many make chemicals to keep from being eaten. Also, plants that grow in shade don't grow as fast. Often they protect their leaves with deadly chemicals.

As rain forests vanish, so do the people who live there. These people know about healing plants. This knowledge is also lost.

Some people work to save that knowledge. They help start school programs. They record local knowledge. They also write books.

▲ This satellite image shows areas of destroyed rain forest.

Untouched Rain Forest

Destroyed Rain Forest

ANTIBIOTICS: PENICILLIN

You know that fuzzy stuff that grows on old food? That is mold. Mold is a fungus. Fungi are decomposers. Fungi break down dead matter. They also take in their nutrients.

The kitchen is the last place you would think to find a life-saving drug. But that is where penicillin (peh-nih-SIH-lin) came from. Finding this drug changed history.

THEY MADE A DIFFERENCE

In 1859, Louis Pasteur showed that bacteria and fungi are in the air. Earlier, doctors thought that nonliving things, like bad air, caused disease.

Pasteur put boiled broth (clear soup) into two containers. He left one container open to the air. He fixed the second container so that air, but not dust, could get in. The open-air broth filled with bacteria. The other broth had none. This helped show that living things cause disease.

▲ Louis Pasteur

18

Penicillin was the first **antibiotic** (an-tee-by-AH-tik). Antibiotics attack bacteria. Antibiotics come from living things. Plants and fungi make these drugs. Some bacteria can also make these drugs.

Bacteria are everywhere. Most are harmless. Some cause serious diseases. They can invade wounds. Before penicillin, even a tiny cut could be deadly. In wars, most soldiers did not die in battle. They died from sickness. Penicillin helped save many lives.

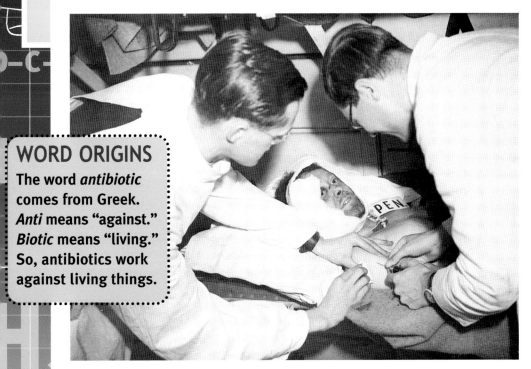

WORD ORIGINS

The word *antibiotic* comes from Greek. *Anti* means "against." *Biotic* means "living." So, antibiotics work against living things.

▲ Penicillin saved thousands of lives in World War II.

LIFESAVING MOLD

In 1928, Dr. Alexander Fleming wanted to study bacteria. First, he had to grow them. He filled plates with a jelly called agar (AH-ger). Then he covered the agar with bacteria.

Fleming saw something odd. A blue-green mold had killed some bacteria. He had found penicillin. Fleming tested the mold in a rabbit. The rabbit lived. Now he knew that the mold did not kill animals. But Fleming did not know which part of the mold killed bacteria.

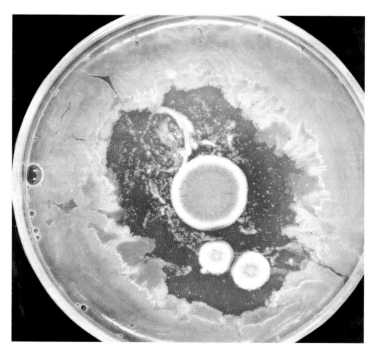

▲ Dead bacteria leave clear circles around antibiotic patches.

In 1939, World War II began. English scientists did an experiment. They infected eight rats with deadly bacteria. They gave four rats penicillin. They did not treat the others. The four rats that got penicillin lived. The other four died. In 1940, the team made their results known.

England was at war against Germany. German air raids blasted English cities. England needed a drug to treat the sick and wounded.

It's a Fact

Even before World War II ended, doctors noticed that penicillin no longer killed some bacteria. The bacteria had become resistant. Today, many more bacteria are resistant to antibiotics.

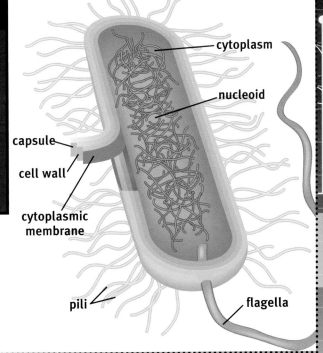

A Bacteria Cell
Bacteria are one-celled organisms.

- cytoplasm
- nucleoid
- capsule
- cell wall
- cytoplasmic membrane
- pili
- flagella

21

PENICILLIN TO THE RESCUE

In 1941, the team tested penicillin on humans. The tests were a success. There was a problem, though. To make penicillin, mold had to grow first. This took time and space. The team used everything they could find to grow it. They even used hospital bedpans. Then chemists had to extract, or take out, the drug. They got very little pure penicillin.

They needed a company to make more penicillin. English drug companies could not make it. Some were working hard on other drugs. Others had been bombed. The team had to find a solution.

HISTORICAL PERSPECTIVE

A moldy cantaloupe is the "great-great-grand-mold" of penicillin. In 1942, scientists in Peoria, Indiana, were studying the drug. They found the melon in a market. The penicillin from the melon mold was very strong. Today, drug companies still grow the mold.

▲ penicillin being grown in 1945

▲ This is penicillin mold.

22

One scientist flew to the United States in 1941. He talked to drug companies. He showed them how to make the drug. Soon, the U.S. entered World War II. The need for a "miracle" drug was greater than ever.

By 1943, twenty-five U.S. drug companies were making penicillin. Almost all of it went to wounded men. Many people worked to make the drug. It was ready just in time.

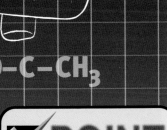

✔POINT

READ MORE ABOUT IT

Would you like to learn about other antibiotics doctors use? Ask your teacher or librarian to help you research this topic in books or on Internet science and medical sites.

▲ A New York drugstore put up this sign in 1945, advertising that they had the wonder drug, penicillin.

HO–C–CH

GROW MOLD ON BREAD

WHAT YOU WILL NEED

- bread without preservatives (bakery bread or homemade bread)
- sandwich-sized zippered plastic bags
- cotton balls
- markers
- notebook

WHAT TO DO

1. First, collect your materials.

2. Next, record the light and temperature conditions of the shelf or countertop where you will store the experiment over the next two weeks.

3. Sprinkle a cotton ball with water. Put it in a bag with a bread piece. Seal the bag and mark the bag with "E" for Experiment, your name, and the date.

4. Place the bag in the chosen storage place.

5. Then put your control piece of bread in a bag with a dry cotton ball. Seal the bag and mark the bag with "C" for Control, your name, and the date. Place it next to the experiment bag.

6. Check the bags each day for two weeks. Record what you see each day.

TALK ABOUT IT

What conditions were best for mold growth? Why did you need a control?

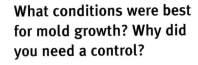

CHAPTER 4

FIGHTING FLU VIRUSES

Every year, fall turns into winter. Then flu strikes. People get fevers, aches, and upset stomachs. In a bad year, up to twenty percent of people get the flu.

Viruses cause the flu. Viruses attack living cells, but viruses are not really alive. Living things consist of cells, but viruses are not cells. Viruses are a few **genes** (JEENZ) packed inside a protein coat.

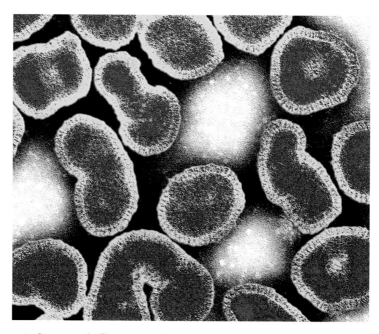

▲ human influenza virus type A

Viruses invade and take control of cells. First, they go into a cell. Then the virus takes over.

The virus tells the cell to make more virus molecules. Those molecules form new viruses. The viruses burst out of the cell and kill it. Then the new viruses infect other cells.

Viruses also mutate (MYOO-tate), or change, very fast. That is why scientists have to make a new **vaccine** (vak-SEEN) for flu each year. A vaccine is a drug made from an old virus. A vaccine protects the body from new viruses.

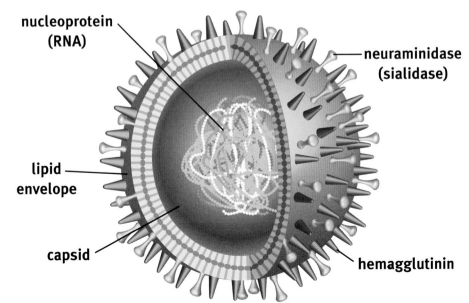

Flu Virus

nucleoprotein (RNA)

neuraminidase (sialidase)

lipid envelope

capsid

hemagglutinin

H₂SO₄

If you get a vaccine for a virus, your body is ready. Your body makes **antibodies** (AN-tih-bah-deez). White blood cells make antibodies. Antibodies fight disease.

A flu shot is a vaccine. When you get a flu shot or have the flu, you become immune (ih-MYOON) to one flu type. That means you will not get sick. But if the virus changes, you may get the flu again.

Flu viruses pass from person to person. Humans can catch the flu from animals, too.

HISTORICAL PERSPECTIVE

In 1918, a bird flu virus jumped to humans. It mutated and spread from person to person. The flu spread quickly around the world. It killed more than 21 million people. A widespread epidemic like this is called a pandemic. Today, pandemics are rare because scientists work to avoid them.

▼ a photograph from the 1918 flu epidemic

Bird flu spread to ▶ Thailand in 2004.

C−O−C−CH₃

CONCLUSION

For thousands of years, people have used plants as medicines. Only in the last few hundred years have we learned how these plants work.

Scientists look for plants and fungi to make medicines. Scientists test these drugs. They see if the drugs are safe for humans.

Twenty-five percent of our medicines come from plants. We need to protect rain forests if we want to find more. People have found 3,000 plants that might be used to fight cancer. About seventy percent of these plants come from rain forests.

Making drugs to fight viruses is especially hard. Viruses change quickly. A vaccine that stops one virus might not stop another.

Scientists study dangerous viruses. They also help chemists make new vaccines. One day, scientists may find a way to stop the spread of the flu.

GLOSSARY

antibiotic	(an-tee-by-AH-tik) a drug produced by an organism that kills microorganisms (page 19)
antibody	(AN-tih-bah-dee) a substance produced by the body's white blood cells to destroy or weaken germs (page 28)
atom	(A-tum) the smallest unit of a chemical element (page 4)
bacteria	(bak-TEER-ee-uh) tiny living cells that cause disease (page 3)
cell	(SEL) the building block of all living things (page 11)
compound	(KAHM-pownd) a substance formed by the chemical combination of two or more elements (page 8)
element	(EH-leh-ment) a substance that cannot be broken down into simpler chemicals (page 4)
fungus	(FUN-gus) decomposer that lives on plant or animal matter (page 3)
gene	(JEEN) a unit that carries the genetic instructions for making cell materials (page 26)
matter	(MA-ter) anything that has mass and takes up space (page 4)
molecule	(MAH-leh-kyool) the smallest particle into which a substance can be divided without being changed chemically (page 4)
nutrient	(NOO-tree-ent) something that is needed by people, animals, or plants for life and growth (page 12)
vaccine	(vak-SEEN) a drug containing dead or weakened germs of a disease that helps the body protect itself against the disease (page 27)
virus	(VY-rus) a tiny, nonliving particle that can invade cells (page 3)

INDEX

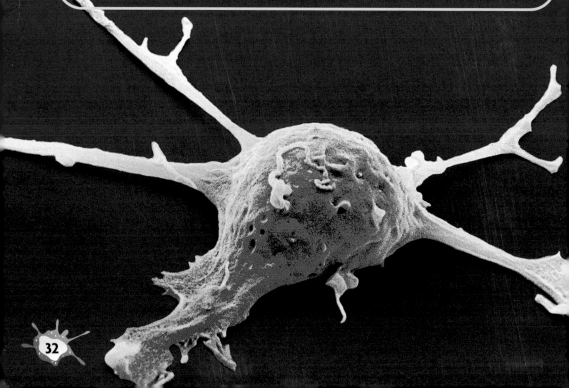